Wh

Birdie L. Muñoz

Illustrated by Mary Ann Zapalac

DOMINIE PRESS
Pearson Learning Group

ISBN 1-56270-468-0

Printed in Singapore
3 4 5 6 7 8   07 06 05

**Dominie
Press**

Pearson Learning Group

1-800-321-3106
www.pearsonlearning.com

Mommy, what's that?

It's a ball.

Mommy, what's that?

It's a shoe.

Mommy, what's that?

It's a picture.

Mommy, what's that?

It's a book. Let's read it.